The Breadfruit Mutiny

Table of Contents	Page

written by Richard Brightfield
illustrated by Stephen Marchesi

McGraw-Hill
School Division

New York   Farmington

The Need For Breadfruit

The year was 1787. Lieutenant William Bligh and his good friend, Fletcher Christian, stood on the shore of the Thames River in London. The sailing ship, the *Britannia*, was moored next to them; it had just brought a load of sugar from the West Indies. During that voyage, which had been commanded by Bligh, Christian had been promoted from a lowly gunner to second mate. The two were discussing a return voyage, when a messenger, dressed in a British sailor's uniform, came running up to Bligh.

"Excuse me sir," the sailor said, out of breath, "but your presence is requested at the Admiralty."

Christian put his hand on Bligh's shoulder. "This could be good news, my friend. This may mean that your commission to the rank of full captain has come through."

"Yes, perhaps it could also be a new assignment," Bligh said.

"Good luck, whatever it is," Christian said.

A short time later, Bligh was ushered into the office of the Lord High Commissioner of the British Navy. The commissioner was sitting behind an oversized oak desk, and flanked by several high-ranking naval officers. The famous English botanist, Sir Joseph Banks, president of the scientific Royal Society of London, was also present.

There was a single chair strategically placed in front of the desk, which the commissioner gestured to and said, "Ah, Lieutenant Bligh, please be seated." As Bligh sat down, the commissioner continued, "I'm sure you know Sir Banks. He was with Captain Cook on his first voyage to the Pacific, as you were on Cook's third and last."

"Sir Banks and I know each other quite well," Bligh replied.

"Sir Banks has requested that you be in command of a very special mission—one of which I highly approve, if truth be told," the commissioner said. "You are to sail to the Pacific island of Tahiti and will purchase a hundred young breadfruit trees; you will then transport them to our West Indian colonies of Jamaica and St. Vincent."

The commissioner turned to the other officers. "I'm sure that Lieutenant Bligh is well acquainted with the breadfruit, but perhaps Sir Banks can fill us in on the details."

"I'd be delighted," Sir Banks said, "as the breadfruit has always been a passion of mine. It grows like apples on large trees—up to sixty feet tall. The fruit, when ripe, is yellow-green, and about a foot in diameter. It has a hard outer husk but is soft and doughy on the inside—like bread. The natives of the Pacific also make a durable paste to use when the fruit is not in season. It requires no work other than climbing the trees to pluck the fruit."

"Thank you, Sir Banks," the commissioner said. "I should also explain the urgency of this undertaking. As you all know, our North American colonies have recently seen fit to reject the authority of the Crown. Up until now, they have been the ones mainly supplying food to our slaves working the sugar plantations of the West Indies. Therefore, a cheap and dependable source of food is urgently needed to feed them. Sir Banks has assured me that introducing the breadfruit to the islands will fill that need."

The BOUNTY Prepares

Lieutenant Bligh met his friend back on the *Britannia*, and explained his new assignment.

"Will I be allowed to accompany you on this voyage to Tahiti?" Christian asked.

"Of course," Bligh said, "I'm to hand-pick the crew, and I've already decided that you are to be the master's mate—third in command. The commissioner told me that he's acquired a three-masted merchant ship, presently being converted to a ship of the Royal Navy. They are also constructing a large greenhouse aboard it."

"A greenhouse?" Christian echoed.

"Yes, well, after the meeting with the commissioner, Sir Banks explained that the breadfruit plants will be carefully looked after by two botanists. They must be protected from seawater at all costs—even from the salty fog that usually accompanies storms at sea. Right now, I suggest we go take a look of this new ship of ours."

The ship, the *H.M.S. Bounty*, was a big disappointment when the two men first saw it. It had a heavy, somewhat squat hull, with three short masts. It did not look any better when they went aboard.

"This looks more like a whaler than an armed transport," Christian said. "I think it's much too small."

"I was told that it's ninety-one feet long and twenty-four feet wide—that's scarcely enough room for a crew of forty-five," Bligh said. "Also, a good deal of space is going to be taken up with a greenhouse that will fill the great cabin from the mainmast to the stern. It's definitely going to be a bit crowded aboard."

"Crowded—I *must* say," Christian said.

"It's not being converted for our convenience," Bligh said, "so we'll just have to put up with it and do the best we can."

"I hope we can keep a crew happy in such a cramped space," Christian said. "Such things can lead to trouble, you know."

The BOUNTY Sets Sail

A month later, the *Bounty* finally left port. Crowded was not the word for it—Bligh's cabin was scarcely six by seven feet! As for the crew, eight-by-ten-foot spaces were screened off below decks. Each of these was home to four of the ship's crew. The men were so cramped that only one at a time could get in or out of his berth.

Despite this, the first week at sea was pleasant enough, but then they were hit by a severe gale, during which the ship sustained considerable damage, especially to its food supplies. Many casks of food on deck were washed overboard and the ship's biscuits, or bread as the sailors called it, were contaminated with seawater.

After two more weeks of stormy weather, the *Bounty* limped into the port of Santa Cruz in the Canary Islands, off the northwest coast of Africa. It spent five days there, with Bligh working the crew hard to repair the ship. None of the crew was allowed to go ashore to see the trim Spanish village of small houses and church spires not far away. Bligh's increasingly frequent outbursts of temper made the crew vaguely aware of what was in store for them in the coming months.

Not long after leaving the Canary Islands, Bligh ordered that a cask of cheese be brought up on deck and opened before the whole crew.

"Aha!" Bligh exclaimed, "I see that one of you scoundrels has stolen two of the cheeses!"

"Excuse me sir," one of the crewmen said politely, "I don't wish to offend you, Captain, but you may remember that you had those two cheeses taken ashore in England."

"You are a liar!" Bligh exclaimed. "One more word out of you, and I'll have you flogged. Furthermore, the cheese allowance for all aboard will be cut in half."

The affair of the cheeses was allowed to drop, but a week later, the store of pumpkins that Bligh had purchased in the Canaries started to spoil. He ordered everyone to eat the pumpkins in place of their bread ration, and there was an immediate protest from the crew.

"I'll have you eat grass or anything else I like!" Bligh shouted at them. "From here on in, anyone who complains about the food will be flogged."

The *Bounty*, under Bligh's command, sailed southwest to the coast of Brazil, then to Cape Horn—the southern tip of South America. The weather changed to cold rain, then to snow and hail. The *Bounty* tried to force its way around the Cape, but was driven back by fierce gales. Sudden, violent lurches of the ship tossed the half-frozen crew around until they were all battered and bruised.

Bligh changed course, and took the ship eastward across the South Atlantic toward the Cape of Good Hope. Assisted by strong westerly winds, the ship soon reached Cape Town at the southern tip of Africa. They stayed there for a little over a month, repairing the ship and restocking supplies.

Then the *Bounty* headed east again toward Tahiti, many thousands of miles away. Finally, ten months after leaving England and having covered 27,000 miles, the *Bounty* arrived at the Pacific island of Tahiti.

During that long voyage, Fletcher Christian had developed doubts about the sanity of his friend, Captain Bligh. Bligh's rages were becoming more frequent, and he'd had men flogged for small infractions. Tahiti, at least, would prove to be a relief.

Tahiti at Last

As the *Bounty* dropped anchor in Matavai Bay, it was greeted by dozens of long Polynesian canoes racing toward it. Soon the decks of the *Bounty* were swarming with native Polynesians.

"Treat the natives kindly," Bligh ordered, "but try to keep them from stealing things."

Bligh relaxed his harsh discipline, and allowed the members of the crew to go ashore. Bligh and Christian soon made friends with Tynah, the native chief. Gifts were exchanged, and the chief helped the botanists from the *Bounty* assemble a garden of breadfruit saplings ashore. This, however, took several months. The crew also had to wait for the proper time to transplant the young trees to the rows of pots in the *Bounty's* greenhouse.

The crew of the *Bounty* made friends with the Tahitians, and soon began enjoying their life there. In fact, a number of the crew wanted nothing more than to stay in Tahiti permanently. After the many months on the beautiful island, discipline was on the verge of breaking down.

The breadfruit seedlings gradually matured, approaching the point where the botanists felt they could be safely transplanted. However, thoughts of mutiny, or rebellion, began to occur among the crew. Three men tried to desert, but were captured and given a dozen lashes each before being put in irons. The rest of the crew still obeyed Bligh's orders...but reluctantly.

The friendship between Bligh and Christian also began to deteriorate. To Bligh's displeasure, Christian was happily living ashore. Things came to a head when Bligh demanded that he turn over a collection of black pearls that Christian had received from the chief. Christian refused to give them up, and from then on, relations between the two became even more strained.

When it was finally time to leave Tahiti, many of the crew were reluctant to go. No one was sadder than Christian. Many friendships had been forged, and when the *Bounty* lifted anchor and sailed out of the bay, the entire population of the island stood on the shore sadly watching its departure.

The Mutiny

As soon as the ship was back out to sea, Bligh was quick to reassert his authority. His bad temper was now, if anything, worse than on the trip to Tahiti. Although a large supply of food had been stored aboard during their stay in Tahiti, Bligh deliberately limited the crew to a small daily ration.

A large pile of coconuts had been stored on deck. Several weeks out, Bligh was inspecting them, when he turned and angrily ordered everyone to assemble on deck.

"Some of you have been stealing coconuts!" he shouted.

"No one has been stealing your coconuts," Christian said. "A while back I may have taken one and I thought it of little consequence. The crew has not taken any."

"One!" Bligh hollered. "You and these other thieving crooks have stolen *half* the coconuts. All of you now have your rations cut in half for the rest of the voyage."

Most of Bligh's tirades seemed to be directed primarily at Christian. Christian began to wonder if the rest of the crew was made to suffer because of Bligh's anger towards him. It was then that he began making plans to desert the ship. He fashioned and hid a crude raft of planks, and waited for the right time to launch it secretly—in fact, many of the crew soon became aware of his plan.

One dark night, Christian was about to launch his raft and set off for a nearby island. Before he could, several members of the crew approached him.

"Christian," one of them whispered, "what you're trying is crazy. Alone, you'll be killed for certain. We have a better plan—we need someone to lead us in taking over the ship. Most of the men will be with you."

Christian thought about it for a while. "All right," he said, "as long as we can do it without bloodshed."

In the distance, thirty miles away across the sea, an active volcano was sending a shower of sparks into the night sky.

The small band of mutineers went quietly to the other crewmembers on watch. They were easily recruited; several had been thrashed by Bligh. One of them had the keys to the arms chest.

At five-fifteen in the morning, as light began spreading in the eastern sky, they went around the ship waking some of the other crewmembers. "Christian is seizing the ship," they whispered, "are you with us?"

By the time the sun had fully risen a little over an hour later, Christian and the others were in total control of the ship. Bligh was still asleep when Christian and two other mutineers, brandishing bayonets, squeezed into his tiny cabin. Christian shook him awake.

"What is the meaning of this?" Bligh demanded, as he opened his eyes.

On his part, Christian's eyes were blazing with revenge. "Hold your tongue!" he said, aiming his bayonet at Bligh's throat. At that moment, Bligh was sure that he was going to be killed. "Murder! Murder!" he began screaming at the top of his voice. Those not with the mutineers thought the ship was being attacked.

There was much confusion throughout the ship. Not everyone was on the side of the mutineers, and for a short time, it seemed that a counter revolt was possible. As for the mutineers, there were several who wanted to kill Bligh then and there. "You gave us empty bellies for the trip," one of them shouted, "now we'll give you a bellyful!" Others wanted to put him in irons and take him back to England. They soon realized, however, that the authorities there would be completely on Bligh's side, and that they would certainly face execution.

Luckily, Christian quickly got things under control. Bligh was allowed to get dressed. He pleaded with Christian to stop the mutiny. "It's too late for that now," Christian said and then gave the order for the ship's launch to be hoisted out. This was the largest boat carried by the *Bounty*. It was twenty-three feet long and a little under seven feet wide. There were no decks, and it was designed to carry a maximum of fifteen men.

Christian allowed the loyalists to stock the launch with supplies. Then after several hours of feverish activity, it was cast off with Bligh and eighteen others. Seven who were still loyal to Bligh had to stay with the *Bounty*.

The Rest of the Story

The crew of the *Bounty*, now under the command of Fletcher Christian, soon tossed all of the breadfruit plants in the ocean. Then, after dropping the loyalists back in Tahiti and picking up some of the Tahitians, they searched for an island where they would be safe. They finally found nearby Pitcairn Island and settled there. Christian had the *Bounty* burned in the harbor.

Bligh and his loyal crewmembers managed to take the overloaded launch 3,600 miles through the islands of the Pacific to Timor, now part of Indonesia. From there, they made it back to England on a Dutch ship.

"Breadfruit Bligh" as he was now jokingly referred to in the British newspapers, was sent to Tahiti again, this time with two ships, and a company of marines. This time he managed to transport breadfruit trees to the West Indies successfully.

The breadfruit thrived in the West Indies, but, after all that work, the slaves there refused to eat it. In 1833, Britain abolished slavery in the West Indies—thirty years before it ended in the United States.